Nigel Stewart

NORMANDY
WAR CEMETERIES

OREP
EDITIONS

INTRODUCTION

Normandy is covered north, south, east and west with war cemeteries. During the summer of 1944, before, on and after D-Day, from the beaches to the streets and through hedgerows, Allied and German forces exchanged bitter blows. Ultimately the battle in Normandy would enable Allied forces to break out towards Paris, Belgium, the Netherlands, Luxembourg and Germany, where the war would end in Europe, converging from all fronts, 337 days after D-Day.

70+ years on, because of D-Day history, the coastline of Normandy is one of the most important tourist destinations in Europe. Along the coast are found several cemeteries that are well known and easily accessible. The Normandy American Cemetery, above Omaha beach, averages at least 1.5 million visitors a year. Nearby, the Bayeux British/Commonwealth cemetery, and the German war cemetery at La Cambe, are also busy places in the summer months.

This guide book is to help the reader locate and visit not just the well-known war cemeteries, but also the lesser known, more numerous and of equal interest, inland from the famous coast of D-Day.

I accept that people want, for understandable reasons, statistics to help as a short-cut to quantify a battle, a cemetery, a war.
When you walk around these places, you gradually forget statistics, reading instead of the age, the name, the epitaphs or the flowers of bereavements or memories of individuals brought together for a cause, for better or for worse.

And the gardens, these burial grounds, now mature in seed 70 years after the war, full of life in fact, are beautifully maintained by all the gardening teams of all the Commissions. Peaceful places…such a contrast to what created them. Lest we forget.

This book is dedicated to all the gardeners of the different war graves commissions, in Normandy and elsewhere.
www.cwgc.org
www.abmc.gov
www.volksbund.de

COLLEVILLE-SUR-MER

Located not far from fields used as a burial area shortly after D-Day (A temporary cemetery had earlier been established beside the beach) the cemetery at Colleville-sur-Mer site was established on land donated by France to the United States. It is exempt of French tax for use in perpetuity as a cemetery. The site was used for relocated burials as of 1948, following the choices of Next of Kin as to whether their loved ones be returned to the United States for final burial or reburied in an American overseas cemetery, in most cases not far from their initial burial sites. Approximately 30,000 Americans died in Normandy – this cemetery and Saint-James representing less than half of that total.

Following virtually all reburials, architecture and landscaping, the cemetery was open to the public in 1956.

Today, the burial count is 9,387 personnel, including 4 women. Latin crosses or Stars of David mark the graves.

There are also 1,557 servicemen whose names are engraved as 'Missing in Action' along the semi-circular wall of the 'Garden of the Missing' - behind the memorial and military maps. One third of the names on this wall, mostly listed as belonging to the

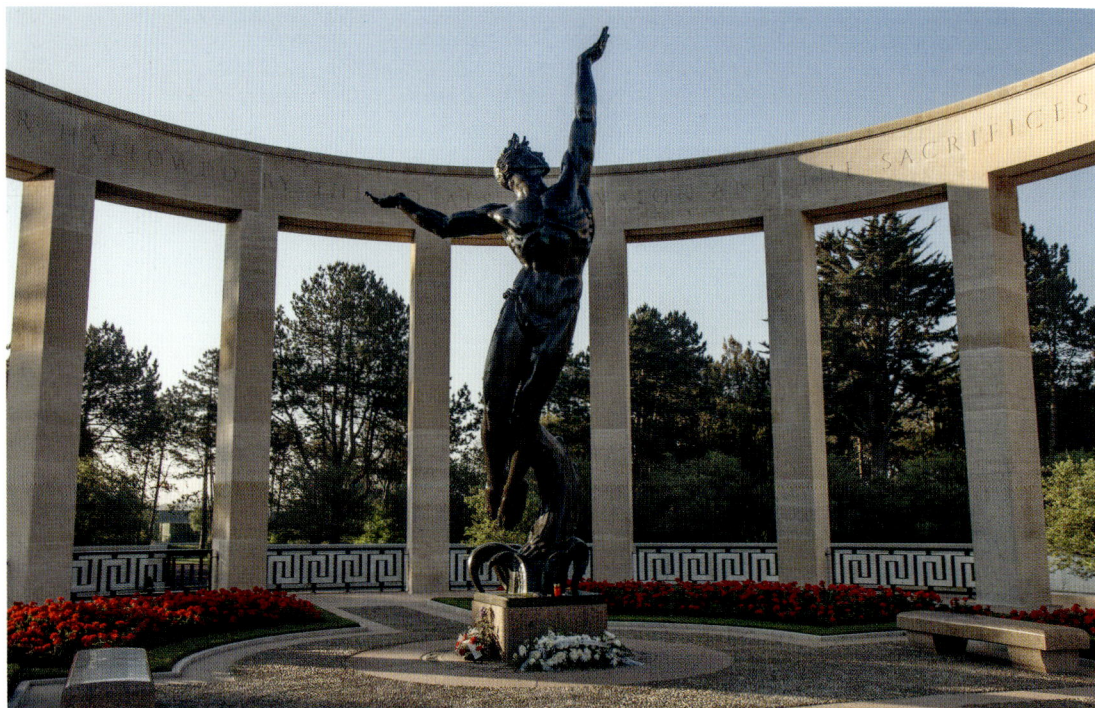

66th Division, were lost with the sinking, by submarine, of the transport ship 'Leopoldville' on December 24th 1944. Many other victims of the attack, whose bodies were recovered the following morning or later, rest in the cemetery.

The bronze memorial statue 'Spirit of the American Youth Rising from the Waves' was sculpted by Donald De Lue, recognized as one of the foremost memorial sculptors of his day. There are 307 'Unknown' soldiers buried among the plots. "Known but to God"... their names will be somewhere on the Wall of Missing.

The 'Dog-Tag' I.D. numbers are engraved on the back base of each marble headstone, unless the casualties were unidentified or were known to be civilians, like War Correspondent, photographer George Bede Irvin (Plot A – Row 12 – Grave 9.) who was accidentally killed, along with many others, by the Allied air bombardment of July 25th 1944, part of Operation 'Cobra'.

Burial plots A to F run from the flags to the chapel. Every other row is numbered on the ground, and the grave number then at the front base of each headstone. Unless the serviceman is known personally or by research, you can find a grave by checking the visitor center data base or through the American Battle Monuments Commission website www.abmc.gov. Next of kin are advised, if they wish, to report to the visitor center desk. The center was opened in 2007 and offers a large exhibit area and several films.

Visitor center

Burial plots behind the central chapel (G, H, I and J) have a large number of servicemen killed between Omaha beach and the fighting inland towards Saint-Lô. Plots in front of the chapel (F, E, D and C) in turn have a large number of burials of servicemen who fought in the Cotentin peninsula.

The front plots A+B, in front of the flags, are more a mix of burials from different dates, including many who died in hospital or in accidents, going into late 1944, 1945 and 1946. All dates of death before June 6 1944 are airmen, except two : Technician 4th Grade Howard Henry and 1st Lieutenant Quentin Roosevelt. Henry, 1st Ranger Battalion, was killed August 19th 1942, during the 'Operation Jubilee' raid at Dieppe. Alongside the predominantly Canadian and British forces involved, were some 50 Rangers at Dieppe, just formed as a WWII elite unit, of whom at least three were killed, including Henry (B.18.5).

Among the burials are 45 sets of brothers that we know of, of which 33 are buried side by side.

A father and son: Father in Normandy, Colonel Ollie W Reed, and son, First Lieutenant Ollie W Reed Jr, in Italy, killed just three weeks apart

(E.20.19 and E.20.20). There are three posthumous Medals of Honor, graves marked in gold letters : First Lieutenant Jimmie Monteith (I.20.12), Technical Sergeant Frank Peregory (G.21.7) and, without a doubt the most visited grave, Brigadier General Theodore Roosevelt Jr (D.28.45). Ropes are often found around the grave here to help grass recover from endless feet on this spot). Roosevelt died of a heart attack a month after leading men ashore at Utah Beach on D-Day. Beside him rests his younger brother Quentin, of the Aero squadrons of World War I, shot down and killed in 1918, buried by the Germans at his crash site at Chamery, just west of Reims, and reburied in Normandy in 1955 alongside his brother. Two brothers, two world wars.

There are two other generals in the cemetery: Brigadier General Nelson Walker 8th Infantry Division (B.23.47) and Lieutenant General Lesley McNair (oldest serviceman here at 61 years: F.28.42.) Posthumously four star General and a key name in America's involvement in World War II, he oversaw the build-up of the army which rose from a small force in 1941 to 8 million overseas at the war's end. On one of the key 'break-out' dates in Normandy, July 25th, the beginning of Operation Cobra, McNair - with scores of others, was killed by Allied air bombardment, too close to the hell unleashed that day from the air, killed by the unfortunately named 'friendly-fire'.

At the back of the cemetery are two statues, one of Columbia and eagle for the United States, one of Marianne and rooster for the French Republic.

Among the burial plots, at the alignment of paths forming a cross, stands the non-denominational chapel, within which is a beautiful ceiling mosaic depicting the journey of Americans by sea and air to Europe, and maternal figures of Columbia and a grateful Marianne.

Date of birth, or age, are not engraved here, unlike Commonwealth or German cemeteries. Whilst not stated, the average age across this cemetery is around 23 years old.

Young lives that gave a lot, and lost everything. Among them Captain Roger B. Dyar (D.27.42) 63rd Fighter Squadron, 56th Fighter group, who was killed in June 1943, shot down in battle over Normandy skies. Just 6 months earlier Roger had, with another man (Lt. Harold Comstock), become the fastest humans on earth, breaking the air-speed record of the time by vertically diving (a 'graveyard dive') their P47, reaching 725 m.p.h - almost at the sound barrier - taking the then conventional planes to their limits. The future was just around the corner…..

Captain Roger B. Dyar

A student of Ohio State University, Roger also wrote poetry :

I wish I might forever stay
Up here with
The Gods at play.
But I am forced
To understand
That I am human
I must land.
(From "Flight")

One of the four civilians buried here, George Bede Irvin (Plot A Row 12 Grave 9) had worked for the Des Moines Register & Tribune in Iowa for eight years prior to moving to Kansas City then Detroit with Associated press.

George Bede Irvin

He came to the U.K. with Associated Press and was accredited war correspondent to the U.S. Ninth Air Force. After landing in Normandy after D-Day at Omaha beach, which had become a logistics staging post, George moved inland and was killed during the July 25th 'Cobra' Allied bombardment.

Lee McCardell of the Baltimore Sun, who was with Irvin that day, said Irvin "apparently hesitated a split second to pick up his camera before diving for a nearby ditch. He was caught in mid air by a bomb fragment and killed instantly." Irvin was found by McCardell crumpled in a ditch, with one camera around his neck and the other lying near an outstretched hand (Van Buren Co, Obituary Keosauqua Public library, Iowa).

BRITTANY AMERICAN CEMETERY,
SAINT-JAMES

GPS: 48.519969, -1.301552

Called "Brittany American Cemetery" even though located in south-western Normandy, near the Mont Saint Michel, this land very quickly became a temporary burial site for war dead immediately following the Avranches breakout: South and east into Brittany and ultimately Brest, south and westwards towards Paris following the German counter-attack on August 7th, attempting to cut Patton's 3rd Army break-out from the northern Allied forces.

Beyond the visitors' reception and superintendent's office is a memorial

E.G. Colvard

building of ecclesiastic style, within which are some wonderful mosaic maps showing the evolution of Allied forces from the Normandy beaches to the war's end.

The burial site itself contains 4,409 young men — average age 22. Among this total, 81 Stars of David, 96 unidentified burials, 21 sets of brothers. Along the wall, beneath the flags, are engraved names of 499 missing in action.

Re-burial completed post-war, after next of kin choices for re-interment either in the United States or in an American overseas cemetery often located near to the war-time burial, the cemetery was dedicated and opened to the public July 20th 1956.

— spent as much time as he could searching for E.G. as the trainloads of wounded were brought in, hoping he was among the injured.

E.G. had in fact been killed after being captured at Pointe du Hoc. He was with other prisoners being transported in a covered truck that was strafed by an Allied plane. A few years ago the Colvard family met a survivor who was by his side when he died, Mr. John Burnett, who escaped from his captors a few days later.

For more information on this and other American Battle Monuments Commission Cemeteries and Memorials, visit: www.abmc.gov

Technician 5th Grade E.G. Colvard, 2nd Ranger Battalion, from Alabama (C.17.12), having scaled the cliff at Pointe du Hoc on D-Day, died some distance inland on June 7th. He was the first son of Early and Eunice Colvard, the eighth child of 14. A star athlete at school, E.G. graduated in 1943, when he was called to military service.

E.G.'s death was a devastating blow to his family, and especially his parents. His father's health failed quickly, and his mother nearly had a nervous breakdown. The family didn't know of E.G.'s fate for almost a year. They received the telegram that he had been killed on April 23, 1945. Previously, they had been told he was wounded, then missing. During that time, his brother Ray (Van Ray Colvard, born October 1924) — serving with the 97th General Hospital in Europe

COMMONWEALTH WAR GRAVES COMMISSION

ROUEN SAINT-SEVER CEMETERY

GPS: 49.412669, 1.069460

One of the largest war cemeteries in Normandy, yet probably the least known despite it's central urban location.

Located in the southern Rouen suburbs of 'Petit' and 'Grand-Quevilly, not far from the football stadium. At the 'Rond Point des Bruyeres' roundabout, take Boulevard Stanislas Girardin. 150 metres further, the communal Saint Sever cemetery entrance is on the left.

During World War I, Rouen was a major logistics area (behind the Somme) for army supply, camps… and several hospitals. The majority in this cemetery died from their wounds in those military hospitals.

As well as over 8,000 burials from WWI, there are just over 300 from WWII, of which some were involved in the Dieppe raid of August 1942. The war cemetery is an extension to the communal cemetery. Prior to arriving in the military burial section, one passes from the civilian communal cemetery to a Rouen WWI

Memorial, sculpted by Charles Verlet, erected post WWI by the city of Rouen: Four women representing the British, French, Italian and Belgian allies of WWI. A semi-circular wall surrounds the memorial with nearly 5,000 citizens of Rouen who died in WWI.

Then one enters the war cemetery, first through French burials, which in turn lead to the Commonwealth War graves area.

Most Commonweath burials are from the UK, Australia, Canada, New Zealand and South Africa, but also numerous headstones are for young men from other countries, notably India and China. There is also a large Commonwealth war cemetery, nearly 2,000 burials, near Le Havre, at the Sainte-Marie cemetery of Graville Sainte-Honorine. Mostly from the First World War, but also some 364 burials from the Second World War. The gps coodinates for this cemetery in Le Havre are : 49.504324, 0.126632

COMMONWEALTH WAR GRAVES COMMISSION

BAYEUX

GPS: 49.274007, -0.713897

The Bayeux war cemetery is the largest Commonwealth cemetery of the Second World War in France.

It is located just outside the town centre, on D5 Boulevard Fabian Ware (named after the founder of the CWGC) very close to the Battle of Normandy museum.

Following Bayeux's rapid liberation June 7th 1944, by a combination of fortunes of war, strategy and location, the town did not suffer the damage inflicted around it. The town quickly became a hub of not just army logistics but civilian refuge. Those arriving from the heavily contested area around Tilly-sur-Seulles found an undamaged town and Cathedral within earshot of outright desolation in their own villages.

With the arrival of logistics, including a large hospital set up just behind this cemetery, came the burial administration, quickly taping out the fields here for the dead that were to increasingly arrive by the truck-load throughout that summer and then winter of 1944 and into 1945. A large number of the dead here were brought from the hospital tents that neighboured this field.

COMMONWEALTH WAR GRAVES COMMISSION

From wartime wooden markers, to the post war landscaping and classical architecture, the cemetery evolved as Europe would in the 50's, from war, to economic recovery through food rations for a decade more, to reconstruction.

The burials total some 5,000 of which 3,935 are from the UK, 181 Canadian, 25 Polish, 17 Australian, 8 New Zealand, 7 Soviet, 5 French, 2 Italian, 2 Czech, 1 South African and 466 German. 388 are unknown burials.

Across the road from the cemetery, engraved on the memorial columns, are 1,809 names of those from the Commonwealth forces who remain 'Missing in Action' in Normandy. The Latin above the names states "We, once conquered by William, have now set free the conqueror's land".

Among the burials, the youngest appears to be Edward William Durn, 48 Royal Marine Commando, aged 17 (XIV.B.15.) who died on D-Day. Indeed, Edward is surrounded by men of his same unit who all died the same day. In Commonwealth cemeteries one can 'read' in the rows of graves, looking at unit and and date, a battle evolution as men were often buried side by side as they were brought in from where they had died. This 'chronology' of burial was lost in American and German cemeteries following post-war reburial.

The age group in this cemetery ranges from 17 to the mid-50's. The British army was stretching itself as the war reached its final year.

Gravestones 'touching': Upon closer inspection one finds the men were in most cases in a vehicle or aircraft…their bodies were often inseperable so were buried together .

Five Victoria Crosses (http://www.historic-uk.com/HistoryUK/HistoryofBritain/The-Victoria-Cross/) were awarded for actions between June and August 1944. One of them, posthu-

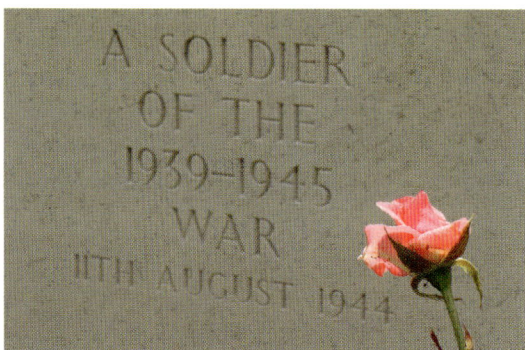

A SOLDIER OF THE 1939–1945 WAR 11TH AUGUST 1944

mous, was awarded to Corporal Sidney Bates, 23, (Grave : XX.E.19), Royal Norfolk Regiment, who died two days after being wounded in the action that would result in the award of his V.C. (https://en.wikipedia.org/wiki/Sidney_Bates).

Large numbers of Commonwealth servicemen were at sea or in the skies of the western American sector of Normandy (erroneously, there is a perception of the Allies divided up into their own areas). Commonwealth dead recovered there were in most cases later brought by truck to the nearest British cemetery to the Americans – Bayeux. Donald Harris (X.A.5.) and John McCoy (X.B.11) were both Royal Navy of HMLCA 914, one of the landing craft involved in the Rangers assault at Pointe du Hoc on D-Day. Just prior to the Rangers landing, before dawn, RAF Lancasters of 50 Squadron bombed Pointe du Hoc. Australians Roland Gilbert Ward (X.A.7) and Malcolm Burgess (X.A.6) were among the men that failed to return from that mission.
(For more details see: http://normandyinsightresearch.blogspot.com)

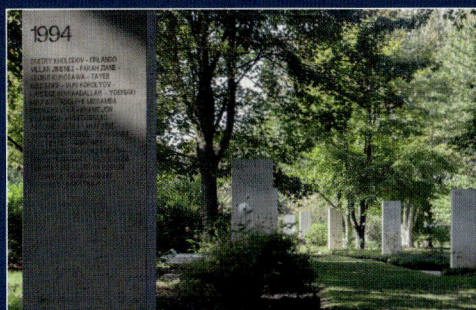

Reporters Memorial

Though not a cemetery, the Bayeux Reporter's Memorial, across the road from the war cemetery has been, since 2007, a worthy addition to remembrance visitation in Normandy, paying homage to the war correspondents from around the world who have died 'reporting war' since the second world war.

http://thejournalistsmemorial.rsf.org/?lang=en

An initiative of the town of Bayeux and 'Reporters without borders' (www.rsf.org), designed by Samuel Craquelin.

Every October, Bayeux hosts a week of conferences, debates and exhibitions about conflict and journalism (www.prixbayeux.org)

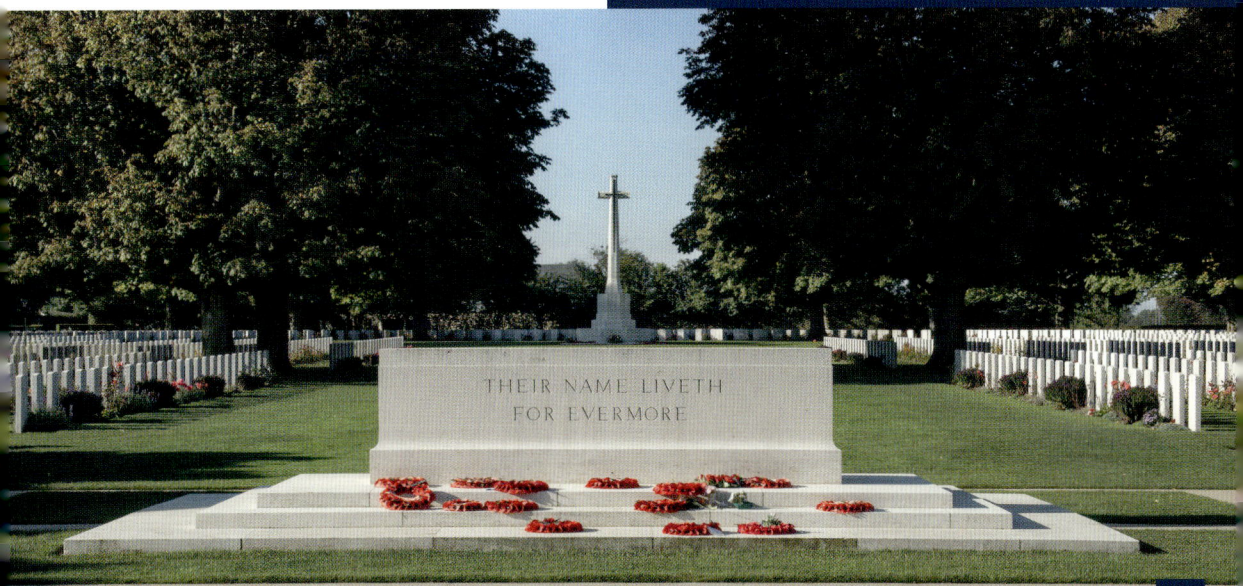

THEIR NAME LIVETH FOR EVERMORE

BÉNY-SUR-MER

GPS: 49.302508, -0.450111

Bény-sur-Mer war cemetery is located just outside the village of Reviers, 4 kilometres inland from Courseulles-sur-Mer, or 14 kilometres north-west of Caen.

The vast majority of burials here are Canadian, and representative for the most part of Canadian units fighting from Juno beach on

D-Day to the attritional battles around Caen.

One of the graves is Anglican Chaplain Captain Walter Brown who, having come ashore on D-Day, administering to wounded and dying on Juno Beach, moved inland

Walter Brown

with the Sherbrooke Fusiliers. In the evening, with two others, Walter's jeep was ambushed near Caen, probably by Waffen-SS units. Initially he was reported P.O.W. Lt. Grainger, in the jeep with Walter, was left for dead but recovered consciousness and drove the still working jeep, with the dead driver, Corporal J.H. Greenwood, back to Canadian lines. With no further news, Walter was 'missing in action'. His body was found by the roadside over

COMMONWEALTH WAR GRAVES COMMISSION

a month later. It appears highly likely from the sole wound to his body, from a bayonet, that he was murdered after being taken prisoner. Walter's grave is located at XIII.C.1.

His communion 'kit', found years later in a charity shop in Windsor, Ontario, was returned to Huron chapel, London, Ontario, where it is still used for remembrance day services.

(information provided by: The Rev. Dr. Tom Wilson, a Canadian Anglican Priest, currently ministering in Scotland).

Total burials in this cemetery, surrounded by maple trees, are 2,049, of which 2,025 are Canadian, 4 U.K. and 1 from France. 19 are unidentified.

BANNEVILLE-LA-CAMPAGNE

GPS: 49.175122, -0.229159

Located some 10 kilometres east of Caen, along the D675 between Giberville and Troarn, the majority of burials here are of servicemen killed from the latter half of July 1944 –'Operation Goodwood'– through to late August, during the encirclements around Falaise and the move towards the Seine. U.K. 2,012, Australia 5, Canada 11, New Zealand 2, Poland 5, Unidentified 140. Total: 2,175 burials.

Among the men buried here is Welsh Guards Lt. Rex Whistler (III.F.22). Rex was an accomplished and recognized artist of his day. In 1927, aged just 22, he completed a mural all around the Tate Gallery Refreshment Room (now Tate Britain). This was recently restored as « The Rex Whistler Restaurant ». On 18.7.44 at the start of Operation Goodwood, his tank became ensnared by wire when crossing a railway cutting. He was killed by mortar fire after dashing across open ground to another tank between the villages of Giberville and Banneville, close to this cemetery. He was 39. His artist and poet brother Laurence (1912-2000) engraved a glass prism in memorial to Rex, which can be seen in the morning chapel of Salisbury Cathedral.

Rex Whistler

BROUAY

GPS: 49.214907, -0.561905

Brouay is a small village located just two kilometres to the south of the N13 road between Caen and Bayeux. The cemetery itself lies just behind the village church. The burial total, in what is probably one of the most tranquil war cemeteries in Normandy, is 377, of which 375 are from the UK. (7 unidentified) and 2 Canadians. Most of those buried here died during the attrition of fighting around Caen through June and July 1944.

CAMBES-EN-PLAINE

GPS: 49.23657 -0.38597

This cemetery lies 7 kilometres north of Caen, in the village of Cambes-en-Plaine (rue du Mesnil-Ricard). Over half the 224 burials here date from 8th and 9th of July, as battalions from the North and South Staffordshire regiments contributed to the final push into the northern side of Caen. The cemetery itself is located on ground that was bitterly fought over for over 4 weeks.

COMMONWEALTH WAR GRAVES COMMISSION

CINTHEAUX GPS: 49.060676, -0.291238

14 kilometres south of Caen, astride the N158 road to Falaise, is located the Commonwealth war cemetery at Cintheaux. The majority of almost 3,000 burials here are Canadian, who for the most part died in the fighting moving out of the south of Caen, towards Falaise, and in the 'Falaise Gap' encirclement of German forces late August 1944.

Every year, local communities gather here on August 8th to commemorate 'Operation Totalize' and the battles that liberated this high ground. It was a key date in the Normandy campaign, coinciding with the German counter-attack at Mortain that was to become the beginning of a vast Allied pincer movement over the following two weeks.

Very much a symbol of this cemetery is Private Gérard Doré (XVI.G.11). Gérard, of Les Fusiliers Mont Royal, was killed July 23rd 1944 in the battle of Verrières ridge. He was in the vicinity of Troteval and Beauvoir Farms that were being used as strongpoints by German forces. He was 16. The chapel at Verrières, not far from Saint-Martin-de-Fontenay, is a commemorative memorial to Gérard and all the Canadians, just one of many 'markers' across Normandy remembering the Canadians who fought and died in the fields around you.

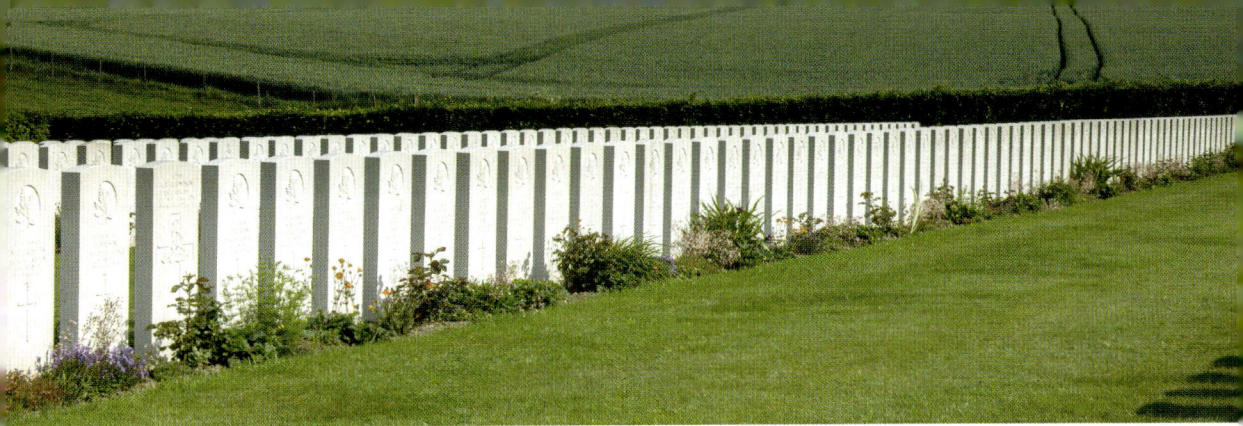

DIEPPE

GPS: 49.896156, 1.068351

Following the evacuations of 1940 and before D-Day, there were numerous raids along the occupied coast of Europe, mostly undertaken by small commando teams. The Bruneval raid, 'Operation Biting' of February 1942, was the first Allied Airborne raid in Europe). Operation Jubilee at Dieppe was the largest of the 'raids'. On 19th August 1942, approximately 6,000 men supported by 250 naval vessels and more than 60 squadrons conducted a "reconnaissance in force". The losses incurred were exceedingly high, with 3,600 killed, wounded and captured.

948 men are buried in this cemetery (187 are unidentified). The majority are Canadian, along with 231 British, 4 New Zealander's, 2 Australians and 1 Indian. Some wounded prisoners later died in captivity and are buried in the WWII section of the otherwise WWI cemetery at Rouen/Saint-Sever.

DOUVRES-LA-DÉLIVRANDE

GPS: 49.290380, -0.376305

Located north of Caen on the D7, this large war cemetery has over 1,000 burials. 927 are from the UK, 11 are Canadian, 3 Australian, 1 Polish and 180 German.

A German-held 'pocket' between 'Sword' and 'Juno' beaches, around the nearby radar station, caused concern for the Allies until its dissolution on June 18th 1944. Douvres was then used as a hospital HQ (in the convent) and fatalities started to arrive here almost immediately.

COMMONWEALTH WAR GRAVES COMMISSION

FONTENAY-LE-PESNEL

GPS: 49.161360, -0.561099

Located 16 kilometres west of Caen along the D139 from Carpiquet, this cemetery has a total of 520 graves of which 457 are British, 4 Canadian and 59 German.

The access remains a dirt road, the cemetery being set back from the main road in the surrounding fields. Thus this ground maintains a feeling of isolation, but is also an extremely peaceful setting. The majority of the dead here fought and died during the bitter fighting of Operation 'Epsom' at the end of June 1944 in the very landscape around you.

Adjacent to the cemetery, on the main road is the 49th (West Riding) Division's "Polar Bear" memorial.

COMMONWEALTH WAR GRAVES COMMISSION

HERMANVILLE-SUR-MER

GPS: 49.286403, -0.308644

From the Sword Beach memorial in Hermanville-sur-Mer, the war cemetery is found by moving inland to "Hermanville-Bourg" on the D60b. The village church is on the left and opposite, a small memorial plaque recounting the use of the village well to provide water for the invasion troops. Just north of the plaque is the "Rue du Cimitiere Anglais". The cemetery is approximately 300 metres down this road.

This war cemetery has many servicemen who died on or around Sword Beach on D-Day and the period that immediately followed in the battle for Caen. The red 3rd Division battle flash insignia is visible on the ground at the cemetery entrance, before passing through the gate into a silence often broken only by birdsong.

1,005 burials. (986 are from the UK, of whom 102 are unidentified), 3 are Australian 3, 13 Canadian and 3 French.)

HOTTOT-LES-BAGUES

GPS: 49.16033 -0.62635

Located on the D9 between Caen and Caumont-l'Éventé, some 15 kilometres southeast of Bayeux, Hottot-les-Bagues war cemetery has more than 1,000 burials. The majority of 1,005 Commonwealth from the UK, but also Canadian, Australian, New Zealand servicemen, as well as a burial section of 132 Germans.

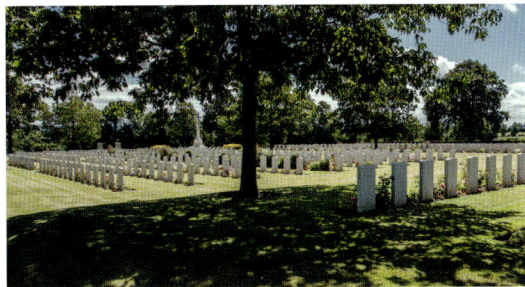

Brigadier James Hargest was from Southland in New Zealand. During WWI he was severely wounded during the Gallipoli campaign in 1915. He would see combat with the New Zealand Division at the Somme in 1916, where actions he took were rewarded with the Military Cross. Leadership of the Otago regiment would later earn him a DSO, a mention in despatches and the Legion d'honneur. In 1931 he became MP for Invercargill NZ, then Awarua in 1935, remaining a seated member throughout WWII. As a Brigadier in WWII, Hargest was among prisoners taken by Rommel's Afrika Korps in North Africa. Escaping with others from Italy in 1943, initially by way of a tunnel, Hargest reached Switzerland, then crossed France to Spain with the aid of the French resistance, reaching England by plane in December 1943. Hargest was appointed New Zealand observer for D-Day, attached to British 50th Division. He died in Normandy having just learnt he was to work with a rehabilitation unit for New Zealander's prior to returning home. A school in Invercargill is named after him. Grave I.C.2.

COMMONWEALTH WAR GRAVES COMMISSION

CHOUAIN – JERUSALEM WAR CEMETERY   GPS: 49.210121, -0.652206

Several of the men buried here died from their wounds in the adjacent farm buildings, used as forward first-aid 'dressing' stations. After the tortuous battle for Tilly-sur-Seulles and the surrounding area, further burials were made elsewhere. This is one of the smallest war cemeteries in France. A miniature version of the other Commonwealth cemeteries, even to the smaller than usual Sword of Sacrifice. There are 47 graves, including 1 Czech. Among them is one of the youngest soldiers to die in Normandy: Private Jack Banks, Durham Light Infantry.

Jack, from Lancashire, was just 16. The bitter epitaph on his gravestone reads "God will tell us why some-day. He broke our hearts and took you away". Two Chaplains are buried here, side by side. Roman Catholic and Church of England. Chaplain Hawksworth had died from injuries sustained when his motorcycle collided with a tank. Chaplain Nesbitt was leading the funeral service for Hawksworth when incoming German artillery killed him too. (#Tom Wilson is currently writing "In the Service of God in the Battle of Normandy". The cemetery is located on the D6 road south of Bayeux, in the direction of Tilly-sur-Seulles.

PUTOT-EN-AUGE   GPS: 49.216585, -0.068496

32 men of the 13th Battalion Parachute regiment buried side by side in the churchyard of Putot-en-Auge, not far from Dozulé, east of Caen, who died in the battle for 'Hill 13' on August 19th, 1944.

RANVILLE GPS: 49.231334, -0.257601

From the famous D-Day site of Pegasus Bridge, follow the D513 eastwards into Ranville village – a short 5 minute drive. The war cemetery is next to the church.

At the heart of the British 6th Airborne D-Day sector, Ranville was the first village liberated, unlike Bréville just up the road that would be bitterly contested for a week more. The first burials were made in the churchyard itself, including Lieutenant Brotheridge, killed crossing the Bénouville bridge during the glider-borne assault on D-Day. (Grave 43).

The adjacent field was then used for continuing the burials that followed during the campaign, and later burials followed at the end of the war from other areas nearby such as Bréville.

COMMONWEALTH WAR GRAVES COMMISSION

AMONG THE BURIALS:

Flight Lieutenant H Lacy Smith (V.F.16.) whose remains and Spitfire were recovered from the nearby river Orne in November 2010. Lacy, 27, had been married just a few months to his English wife. Lacy was interred in Ranville in 2011. The Spitfire is now in Australia. (http://airpower.airforce.gov.au/ Publications/Details/608/On-Laughter-Silvered-Wings-A-Biography-of-Henry-Lacy-Smith.aspx)

R.E. Johns (13th Bn South Lancashire Regiment, Parachute Regiment.) who was just 16.

Two Canadian brothers, side by side : Maurice and Philippe Rousseau, 1st Canadian Parachute Battalion, graves : VA.G.7 and VA.G.8.

A large number of men here are 6th Airborne Division. However, many others here are from units that landed at Sword beach to be moved through Bénouville as re-inforcements for the easternmost Allied sector, one that was a 'blocking' flank until the south and east moves of operations 'Goodwood' and 'Paddle' of July and August 1944.

Total burial is over 2,500, of which 2,151 U.K., 76 Canadian, 2 Australian, 1 from New Zealand, 1 Belgian, 5 French, 1 Polish and a plot for over 300 Germans.

RYES

GPS: 49.299689, -0.600974

Bazenville-Ryes war cemetery can be reached either by following from Arromanches the D87 then crossing the D112, the cemetery is on top of the hill, just ahead. Or by heading from Bayeux to Sommervieu along the D12 then the D87.

Burials first took place here just two days after D-Day and the landing of British 50th infantry at Gold beach, then continued as land was gained and more dead recovered. Burials total is 988, including 652 Commonwealth — of

which 630 U.K. (58 unidentified), 1 Australian, 21 Canadian, 1 Polish and 335 Germans (60 unidentified) — Allied units recovering German dead first, as advance was made.

SAINT-CHARLES-DE-PERCY

GPS: 48.927666, -0.802189

Located in south-western Normandy in an area strangely overlooked or not associated with British units, most burials here were from the hedgerow fighting of late July to early August, in the push towards Vire. Total burial is 809 of which: U.K. 790 (104 unidentified) / Canadian (2 unidentified) and 2 Australians.

SAINT-DÉSIR-DE-LISIEUX

GPS: 49.139655, 0.164175

Neighbouring a German war cemetery (a small path and gate divides the two) the Saint-Désir Commonwealth war cemetery is located just west of Lisieux at the entrance northwards of the D159 connecting with the Lisieux-Caen D613.

600 burials, of which the majority died in the move east to the Seine, through devastated areas like Pont-l'Évêque and Lisieux. But also nearly 100 (RAF) brought from Chartes after the war. There are also 4 First World War burials. 569 British, 16 Canadians, 6 Australians, 5 South Africans, 1 New Zealander, 1 American. For a brief moment in April, cherry blossom turns this war cemetery into an explosion of colour.

COMMONWEALTH WAR GRAVES COMMISSION

SAINT-MANVIEU

GPS: 49.177030, -0.513974

Saint-Manvieu – Cheux war cemetery is located 10 km west of Caen, following the D9 from Carpiquet.

The area between Tilly-sur-Seulles to the south-west of Caen and the battles for 'Hill 112' saw several weeks of attrition following D-Day until late July 1944. Most of the dead buried here are from those weeks.

Of the 1,627 Allied burials, all but two (1 Canadian, 1 Australian) are British. There are also 550 German soldiers.

With the passing of the 70th anniversary of D-Day, it will shortly become a thing of the past to see and meet the veterans that returned here so regularly the last thirty years. Away from the ceremonies and get-togethers, they visited their friends who remain buried here, like Corporal Ronald Millington, who returned to Saint-Manvieu cemetery in 2001 to pay his respects and salute his friends, his comrades, his brothers in arms, Signalman Edward Russell, 43rd Wessex Division and Lieutenant-Colonel William Blacker, Royal Artillery, both killed the same day during the no-man's land battle of Hill 112 , July 11th 1944. Ronald himself passed away in 2011 aged 101.

SECQUEVILLE-EN-BESSIN

GPS: 49.234387, -0.508122

A veritable battlefield cemetery set in a landscape that though peaceful now, still has a no-man's land feel about its open vast plains around Caen.

Located between Caen and Bayeux, 4 kilometres north of Bretteville-l'Orgueilleuse, the cemetery is found just east of Secqueville-en-Bessin on a still small road towards Lasson. The cemetery itself is a dead end road where a total of 99 British and 18 Germans are buried together at rest where they once fought one another.

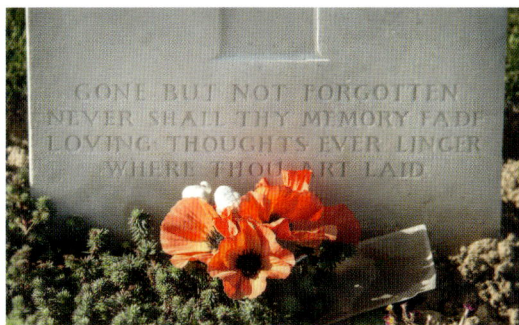

COMMONWEALTH WAR GRAVES COMMISSION

TILLY-SUR-SEULLES

GPS: 49.173918, -0.638127

Located on the D13, 1 km west of Tilly-sur-Seulles, 13 km south of Bayeux, this cemetery has a total burial of 1,200, the majority at 990 being British, plus 2 Canadians, 1 Australian, 1 New Zealander and a plot for 232 Germans. The intense fighting between British and German forces, throughout June and July 1944, in and around Tilly-sur-Seulles, for control of the north-south east-west road network, brought high losses, both military and civilian.

After the war Tilly-sur-Seulles was almost completely rebuilt and is an example of the post-war renconstruction style of housing in this part of Normandy.

Among the graves, Captain Keith Douglas, recognized as one of the great war poets of his generation. His poems have come to symbolize the generation born of the first world war that grew through the depression to fight the second conflict, his style

COMMONWEALTH WAR GRAVES COMMISSION

'impressionist' of the human condition within the mechanization of conflict.

Keith had served in Palestine and North Africa from 1941 to 1943, before landing in Normandy. He was killed from shrapnel on 9th June 1944, having passed through Bayeux to the front, to Cristot, not far from Tilly sur Seulles. Age 24. Grave I.E.2.

Vergissmeinnicht

Three weeks gone and the combatants gone
returning over the nightmare ground
we found the place again, and found
the soldier sprawling in the sun.

The frowning barrel of his gun
overshadowing. As we came on
that day, he hit my tank with one
like the entry of a demon.

Look. Here in the gunpit spoil
the dishonoured picture of his girl
who has put: *Steffi. Vergissmeinnicht.*
in a copybook gothic script.

We see him almost with content,
abased, and seeming to have paid
and mocked at by his own equipment
that's hard and good when he's decayed.

But she would weep to see today
how on his skin the swart flies move;
the dust upon the paper eye
and the burst stomach like a cave.

For here the lover and killer are mingled
who had one body and one heart.
And death who had the soldier singled
has done the lover mortal hurt.

Keith Douglas
(Vergissmeinnicht – Forget-me-not.)

COMMONWEALTH WAR GRAVES COMMISSION

TOURGÉVILLE

Tourgéville war cemetery is located inland from Deauville, following the 'Rue du Moulin Saint Laurent' uphill until the 'Chemin du cimetière militaire'.

Deauville/Trouville was a military hospital area in 1917/18. This war cemetery has 210 Commonwealth burials from WWI and 13 from WWII. Additionally, 90 Germans are buried here from WWII, many having died on June 6th 1944. Not far from here, the German coastal battery at Mont Canisy was heavily neutralized by Allied air and naval forces.

EPITAPHS

Statistics are forgotten when reading the epitaphs on the majority of Commonwealth gravestones.

Following both World Wars, the Commission invited parents or widows, in some cases husbands, to choose a suggested epitaph of a hymn, prayer, or something more personal. Limited to 66 letters, at a cost of 3 ½ pence per letter, this initially compulsory price was later changed to "Voluntary donation if possible".

The words engraved often evoke intense emotion, from sadness, pride to anger, but are silent, waiting to be read and felt, not shouted. The epitaphs make any Commonwealth cemetery visit one remembered by not just the environment but the poetry of words engraved.

URVILLE-LANGANNERIE

GPS: 49.023364, -0.269934

Located on the N158 road from Caen to Falaise (exit Urville), this cemetery represents the dead of 1st Polish Armoured Division, excluding some that died in 1940. There had been Polish Airborne, Naval and Air-force units present on D-Day and thereafter (Burials in Commonwealth cemeteries), but the arrival of the 1st Armoured Division at Arromanches in August 1944 marked the arrival 'en masse' of the Polish on the battlefield.

As part of Canadian 1st Army, it was deployed during 'Operation Totalize' on August 8th 1944 in the move south of Caen. Two weeks later, holding the 'gap' in the encirclement of German forces, between Saint Lambert and

•MORT POUR LA PATRIE•

Chambois – "The death corridor" – the Polish fought with desperate German forces, in front of them and behind. The Polish Division endured over 2,000 casualties killed and wounded in that short time.

Commonwealth authorities moved the Polish dead to this ground near Urville, and oversaw maintenance until French authorities took over in 1949.

This cemetery rightly gives testament to the contribution of a nation ripped to shreds by WWII, and of the loss of the Polish contribution to the Allied coalition.

Poland's fate was settled the moment the Hitler-Stalin non-agression pact was signed in August 1939. Sealed until 1991, when Soviet forces left Poland at last to its own self-determination.

Fittingly, this cemetery lies close to important Polish immigrant communities in the area between Potigny and Mondeville, which, before and after WWII, found work in the local mining and steel industries.

Burials : 615 total, of which 27 unidentified, 4 Jewish, 97 « Empty places » (From the Polish - Missing in Action).

GERMAN WAR GRAVES COMMISSION (VOLKSBUND)

LA CAMBE

GPS: 49.342091, -1.026496

More than 4,000 Americans had been buried here by late July 1944, mostly from the battles in the move on Saint-Lô. 1,880 German dead had been buried too, and after the war, with the Americans reburied elsewhere, the fields here were used again, first by French authorities, then German, for re-burial of Germans from some 1,500 burial sites across the region.

Originally conceived as a cemetery for approximately 8,000, there are more than 21,300 men buried at La Cambe. The total number gradually increases, as this cemetery is still used when German war dead, the missing, are recovered in excavation or agricultural work across Normandy.

Most of the landscaping and architecture was made between 1958 and 1961, when the cemetery was opened to the public.

The burials are in collective groups and the majority of the flat concrete markers have two names for the burials either side. Indeed, the burial density of this cemetery, proportional to acres, is very high.

The 5 small basalt crosses repetitively spaced across the cemetery, amongst the graves, are ornamental.

GERMAN WAR GRAVES COMMISSION

'Ein Deutscher Soldat' is an unknown soldier. Sometimes you will see 'Zwei' or even 'Drei' on one marker, for two or three unidentified men buried together. Approximately 22% of those in the cemetery remain unidentified.

Some of those buried here died in the campaign in 1940, some from the occupation and some from after the war (PoWs who died from accident or disease) but the majority are from the Battle of Normandy.

Many names are not 'German' but from eastern European states. Polish or Czech for example, due to alterations of national boundaries, but also Soviet nationals who served in the Wehrmacht for personal reasons, political –

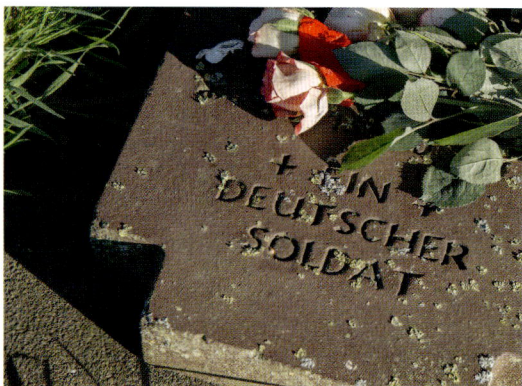

anti-communist, or those who saw Germany as a chance to return to independent states rather than the Soviet Union.

Entering the cemetery through a door designed for one person at a time, one is briefly alone in front of 21,000 who cannot talk. The visitor sets eyes on the central mound which was made in 1958. At the top, a cross and either side a woman and man in bereavement for a son or brother. At the base of this 6 metre mound, often the place for ceremonies, an engraved poem ends with the words « God has the last word ». Beneath this mound lie another 296 soldiers, of which 207 are unknown.

Among the burials in this cemetery is General Major von Dawans (Block 30 Row 10 Grave 400), who was killed, with several of his staff, on June 10th 1944, when the headquarters of Panzer Group West at La Caine, south of Caen, was attacked by the RAF. The location of this headquarters had been determined following 'Enigma' interception by 'Ultra', at Bletchley Park. (http://www.bletchleypark.org.uk)

Many visitors here will have been to La Pointe du Hoc, not far from here. Bombed several times before D-Day, on April 25th 1944 men

like Otto Keller (Block 35 Grave 100) died there from the bombardments that resulted in the relocation of the guns away from their cliff-top positions. It appears likely, given dates of death, that others buried around Otto were killed during the same bombardment.

The small visitor centre in the car park is excellent and offers more information about not just German war cemeteries maintained by the Volksbund commission, but Allied as well. Running along the road to and surrounding much of the cemetery are approximately 1,224 maple trees, which since 1996 are 'named' following a substantial donation to the commission, which as a charitable association relies primarily on private donation for the maintenance of these grounds and the hundreds of others across the world. The last twenty years have seen a huge increase in German war cemeteries after the opening up of territories of the former Soviet Union. Thousands of soldiers each year are reburied from scattered fields to cemeteries such as this.

www.volksbund.de

GERMAN WAR GRAVES COMMISSION

CHAMPIGNY-SAINT-ANDRÉ

Originally a location first used by the Americans, who buried their dead and the Germans in two neighbouring fields.

This cemetery, south of Evreux, is located far from the tourist route of WWII history in Normandy, and thus often a very quiet place to visit. Yet it is one of the largest cemeteries, with 19,836 burials.

The majority of dead were recovered from eastern Normandy's Seine region following the Allied advances in August 1944, but there also war dead here that had first been buried in or near Paris during the occupation.

Among the burials : Oberfeldwebel Karl Daniel, Rommel's chauffeur on July 17th 1944. Returning from the front south of Caen, RAF 2nd Tactical Air Force strafed Rommel's car on the road between Livarot and Ste.Foy de Montgommery, in the direction of Vimoutiers. Rommel was badly wounded and would live until October 1944. Karl died several hours after the attack. Block 10 Row 10 Grave 665.

Field Marshal Erwin Rommel and – in all probability – his chauffeur Oberfeldwebel Karl Daniel.

GERMAN WAR GRAVES COMMISSION

SAINT-DÉSIR-DE-LISIEUX

GPS: 49.139655, 0.164175

Perhaps the most overlooked part of the Battle of Normandy, (overshadowed by the Falaise Pocket 'Death corridor') is the move eastwards through the Pays d'Auge, Lisieux to Rouen, and the blockade siege and destruction of Le Havre.

This German cemetery neighbours a British-Commonwealth cemetery (597 burials) and the two can, fittingly, be visited side by side, through a gate.

Opened in 1961, the total burial here is 3,735 war dead.

Unlike the flat grave markers of La Cambe or Marigny, the grave markers here are red sandstone crosses, names on each side, again a 'collective' grouping in burial.

Two brothers lie in this cemetery, killed not far from each other on 9th August, Hans Baumann (Block 3, Row 22, Grave 697) and 16th August, Werner Baumann (Block 3, Row 42, Grave 1,304)

GERMAN WAR GRAVES COMMISSION

HUISNES-SUR-MER MONT D'HUISNES

GPS: 48.615589, -1.453109

Not so far from the American cemetery at Saint James, the German cemetery (Ossuary) at Mont d'Huisnes, is located on a 30 metre hillock near the bay of the Mont Saint Michel. The view of the Mont Saint Michel from the top of this ossuary is superb.

Post war, here were brought the German dead, in majority, from a first burial in regions surrounding Normandy – Brittany, Loire, Mayenne – and the Channel Islands – which had a German garrison under blockade that did not take formal surrender until May 9th 1945.
Total war dead: 11,956.

MARIGNY

Another German cemetery that was first used by American authority to bury its dead, and German dead, that had been killed in the 'Bocage' gridlock. Some American units were within 5 miles of Saint-Lô by June 13th. It would take another month to move through those last five, in the labyrinth of the surrounding hedgerows.

The German war graves commission started relocating its dead here in 1957, from numerous war burials in this area.

Like La Cambe, the grave markers here are flat with, generally, two names on each, or unknown. Also like La Cambe, groups of crosses (3 here not 5 like La Cambe) are dispersed across the burial in an ornamental manner.

The total burial is 11,169.

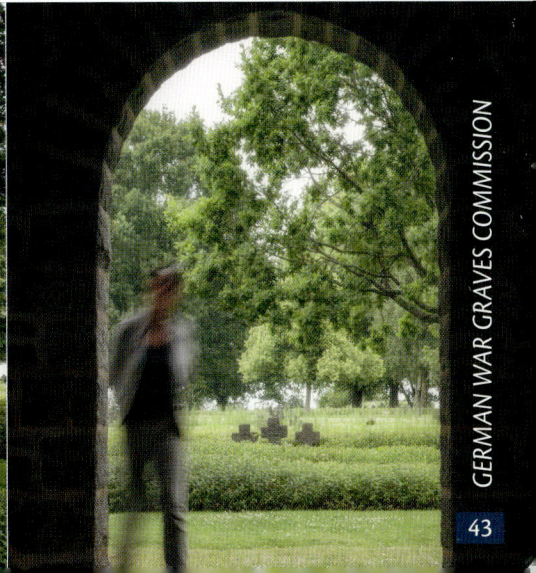

GERMAN WAR GRAVES COMMISSION

ORGLANDES

Curiously not a well known cemetery, given its closeness to such a heavily visited town

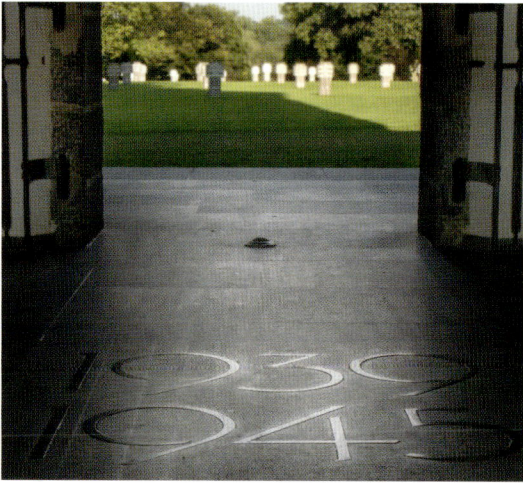

as Sainte-Mère-Église, the German war cemetery at Orglandes, a tiny village, contains 10,152 dead.

One grave marker has 22 names on it — Prisoners of War killed in a dynamite explosion near Bayeux in October 1945 — buried together — Block 27 Row 13 Grave 420/421.

General Wilhelm Falley, commander of 91st LuftLande-Infanterie Division, was the first German General to die as D-Day began operations in Normandy, killed in an incidental ambush in the first early hours of June 6th when returning to his headquarters at Picauville. Block 10 Row 2 Grave 207.

GERMAN WAR GRAVES COMMISSION

ISOLATED CWGC BURIALS

Many churchyards and communal cemeteries in Normandy hold the remains of hundreds of servicemen that died during WW II. The majority are airmen, some are commandos. They died in operations from 1940 to beyond D-Day.

Not buried in the 'principal' cemeteries that followed Operation Overlord, they were left where they were buried either during the occupation or after.

A green metal "Commonwealth War Graves" plaque on the wall of a churchyard or other cemetery – approximately 360 in Normandy alone – indicates an individual or small group of graves, the temporary wartime marker now replaced with the familiar Commonwealth headstone.

The Commonwealth War Graves Commission smartphone app "War Graves" can locate, using geo-localisation, any of the 'isolated burials' wherever you are, simply by searching on "cemeteries nearby".

NECROPOLE LES GATEYS

GPS: 48.507848, 0.063470

Uniformed French personnel were present with the Allies on D-Day and thereafter. French burials can be found in many Commonwealth cemeteries alongside the Allied units they were serving with. But the uniformed French presence in Normandy became substantial following General Leclerc's 2nd Armoured Division's arrival on August 1st 1944, from Africa via re-supply in the U.K, to be part of General Patton's 3rd U.S. Army Group. French soldiers that died in Normandy were in their majority buried near to their families, which was not just metropolitan France, but also Colonial France. In this small cemetery you will find Christian Jewish and Muslim casualties remembered. 6 were buried here following combat in these forests in 1944. In 1964 the 2nd Armoured veterans association purchased the land. In 1987 11 more men were re-buried here.

CIVILIAN VICTIMS IN NORMANDY

It is difficult to give an accurate figure for civilians who died in Normandy in 1944… on which date does one stop ? Are those who died of wounds or injuries weeks or months later to be included…The pre-D-Day allied 'transportation' bombardments were of an area much larger than just Normandy. At least 20,000 died during the spring and summer of 1944 in Normandy. At least three times that many were wounded. Booby traps,

strafing and bombardment, deportation or execution. These civilians were, by July 1944 in Normandy, outnumbered in population by the combatants of both sides. From village to city, the WWI monuments of the 1920's, with the endless lists of those that did not return to their communities, were altered after WWII to include the military deaths of 1939-45 and 'Victimes Civiles'.

To not forget the rest of France, Allied bombardments from Calais to Bordeaux probably accounted for at least three times more this figure. The price of liberation from a total war was very high, and of course remains so for civilians across the world.

This memorial in the Saint Gabriel communal cemetery of Caen, by Charles Lemarouier, is dedicated to the civilians who died in Caen.

ACKNOWLEDGEMENTS

I would like to thank the following people for their help in the creation of this book:
Christine Stewart, Orep Editions, Alain and Nathalie Dupain, ABMC, CWGC, Volksbund, Sean
Claxton www.normandyinsight.com, Geert Van de Bogaert www.normandyheroes.com, Lucien
Tisserand, Ohio State University, Faber & Faber, The Australian Embassy in Paris, Kathy Rooks-
Denes, Dennis Dostine, Alf Batchelder, Damien Maury-Tarriet, Desmond Graham & the estate of
Keith Douglas, Anaelle Ferrand, Sally Hunt, Mike Rowley, Hal Buell, Associated Press, James
Hargest & The James Hargest College, Invercargill, New Zealand, Daniel Whistler, Tom Wilson,
Cy & Alison Percival, Jacqueline and Ian Stewart.

INDEX